D0532656

most of
weddings

A practical guide for churches

Andrew Body

CHURCH HOUSE
PUBLISHING

Church House Publishing
Church House
Great Smith Street
London SW1P 3NZ
Tel: 0207 898 1451
Fax: 0207 898 1449
ISBN 978-0-7151-4125-0

Published 2007 by Church House Publishing

Cover design by ie Design
Printed by Creative Print and Design Group, Blaina, Wales

Contents

Foreword

The knee-jerk reaction of some people to any new idea is to raise questions, see difficulties, think of problems, and be generally discouraging, whether they mean to or not. By contrast, others show a 'can do' mentality that is encouraging and warming, welcoming the opportunity that is presented.

In this immensely practical and stimulating book, Andrew Body encourages the Church in the positive, 'can do' mentality. Joyful and dignified weddings bring exciting opportunities, above all for the couple themselves, but also for their families, friends and, not least, the mission of the Church.

Marriage is absolutely fundamental to our human life and, therefore, to society's health. Couples need every possible help and encouragement to walk this path. The Church is brilliantly placed to provide that assistance. However well priests and congregations fulfil their ministry to couples and their families, there is always room for improvement and development. Andrew rightly stresses the need to make the most of follow-up opportunities after the wedding, and to be 'culture critical' in offering ways of taking the commercial hype and expense out of wedding days.

There is a great deal here to encourage and help all congregations to assist couples at the start of their married life so that they continue to grow in love and their homes become places of love, security and truth. Read on …

+Anthony Hereford

Introduction

This book sprang from a suggestion I made on behalf of the Trustees of FLAME (Family Life and Marriage Education) at our regular consultation with the Mothers' Union that we might cooperate on a leaflet of 'Good Ideas for Weddings'. Whilst the idea was warmly welcomed, we soon realized that there was much more to be said than could be contained in a leaflet, and so we approached Church House Publishing about producing something more substantial. They also warmly welcomed the idea, and this book is the end result.

I am very grateful to the FLAME and MU networks for their cooperation. They both asked for contributions from their members, and I was delighted by the variety and imagination that parishes are showing up and down the land. Originally I had intended to indicate where each of the ideas came from, so that readers could make contact if they wanted more details. But it soon became apparent that that would be impossible. Some ideas were sent in from several different places, and it would be wrong to name one and not all. Some I have to own as my own suggestions, but they are amongst the least imaginative!

This book is for anyone in parishes who wants to develop their ministry to people getting married and their families. No one can do all the things suggested in this book – and would be crazy to try. But, hopefully, as you read through, from time to time you will say, 'We could do that!'

The shape of this book

We start by exploring the tremendous opportunity that weddings present to churches in their mission. We are in a new and more competitive market, and should be out there telling people what a good product a church wedding is. We then trace the process through from the first contact couples make to what happens after the marriage.

The last two chapters are rather different. One gives an account of how two specific parishes have risen to local opportunities and challenges. I am very grateful to them for sparing me time to explain what they are doing. The last chapter is about more radical attitudes – ways in which we can get away from the rampant commercialism that surrounds weddings, and perhaps make them both cheaper and more ethical.

I hope you will find this book a stimulus to a fresh look at weddings to see how this aspect of parish life can be developed. It is such a privilege to be involved with people at an important time in their lives. We can all do it better – and sharing other people's good ideas and experiences ought to help that process. I have learned a great deal as I have been writing this book. I hope you will too.

1 Opportunities and attitudes: making the most of weddings

The Church's greatest home mission opportunity

There is no greater mission opportunity for the Church today than a wedding. Not only does a couple come wanting something from us, and open to what we can offer, but most of the people who gather for the service will never step inside a church for any other reason. In a country that is largely 'unchurched' this is a moment, however brief, when people experience what the church *does* rather than what it looks like, what it *is* rather than what it is perceived to be. It is sometimes difficult for church people, for whom services, prayers, hymns and clergy are part of their weekly experience, to remember how alien this is for the majority, who haven't sung hymns since they were at school, and who may never have spoken to a priest in their lives.

Quite rightly we talk about the Church's mission in terms of going out to where people are in their work and leisure activities. But on this occasion they are coming to us. Here is a heaven-sent opportunity we must grasp to communicate something of what we believe about God and his love. What we make of it will affect how those people think of the Church. Hopefully, it will be a bridge-builder leading them to hear more of the gospel.

For most couples, too, a church service will be a new experience. They may have chosen a church wedding for all sorts of reasons – family tradition or a desire for a good setting for photographs at one extreme, right through to a need to express a sense of the transcendent at the other. They may not be able to articulate such a deep-seated feeling, but it is often there, expressed in words such as, 'It wouldn't seem right anywhere else.' And they will talk of 'churches having a lovely atmosphere'. We need to be listening to the meaning behind the words, and not be getting worried if the couple are not using the traditional religious vocabulary that we are so familiar with.

Whatever the reasons for their request to get married in church, we are given an unparalleled opportunity to help the couple articulate their spirituality, and to relate the Christian faith to their lives.

The new context in which we work

Weddings are now big business, and this is a competitive market place. In previous generations the Church did not have to worry about competition because the choice was either the local church or a very often rather depressing and uninspiring office in a municipal building. Now couples wanting to tie the knot can look to stately homes and castles, as well as package deals in magnificent hotels or the increasingly affordable option of jetting off for nuptials on a white sandy beach washed by warm ocean waves.

Venues that are second to none

But the fact remains that couples want to get married somewhere, despite the gloomy forecasts over the years about marriage being a dying institution. In this world of choices, we have a responsibility to make the church option the most attractive of all. We have a tremendous start in having throughout the country venues that are second to none. Many of them are extremely old, and some couples find that their own sense of making history on their wedding day is fed by celebrating it in a building steeped in history. In my own church, three of the eight bells are five hundred years old. The thought of all the couples for whom those bells have pealed puts the whole event on another plane.

But ancient or modern, our buildings are purpose-built for acts of worship, which is what we are offering to a couple getting married. We are setting their love in the context of the eternal love of God. A building that has been designed for this purpose has a head start over any room in a town hall or, indeed, in a castle. As I have already mentioned, many couples whose attachment to the church is negligible, when entering into such a profound act as getting married, have a deep-seated need to make it transcend the legal and the social. Our buildings are a means of articulating the transcendent for them, however vague their faith may be.

People who are second to none

Not only do we have wonderful buildings, we have wonderful people. The principle is the same. Registrars may do an excellent job, but they are earth-bound. A priest is offering, by his or her role, an opening into the sacred. A parish priest is someone who is in touch with human life at its best and its worst, someone who is privileged to enter into the lives of families at all the major crisis points. And with the parish priest comes a whole army of others who add their skills – and often very considerable skills – to enhance the event with flowers and music.

All this we provide at a very small cost. It would be sad if church wedding fees ever approached the levels charged at secular venues. We are proclaiming the concern of God for each of us in our lives and relationships. It is part of being the servant church that we are there for people in their need. So not only do we have great venues and skilled personnel – we provide them at a bargain rate. The marriage industry encourages people to spend vast amounts on the wedding 'peripherals'. By avoiding the rampant commercialism we proclaim an alternative world-view. That can be made more apparent if we find ways of promoting marriages that are not a threat to bank balances. This will form the subject of a later chapter.

Positive attitudes

The problem with keeping charges down is that we can fall into the trap of not valuing highly enough all that we offer. We can do it better than secular venues – and we need to have the confidence to sell our product with enthusiasm. But here we begin to touch on a variety of attitudes to be found not only amongst clergy, but amongst PCCs and churchgoers in general. There are churches where the ministry to couples getting married is approached with energy and delight, but at the other extreme are clergy who see non-churchgoing couples claiming their legal right to a wedding in their parish church as an imposition on their time – time that could be spent more profitably in other ways – and congregations who resent the invasion of their premises by people who don't quite know how to behave in church. Their attitude is negative. Instead of privilege and opportunity, they see exploitation.

Those are extreme positions, and probably most of us are somewhere in the middle, or find ourselves veering from one direction to another. I want to argue that whatever feelings may predominate, we need to see that weddings are wonderful opportunities. But it is not a question of 'using' the opportunities simply to recruit new members for the church. To use weddings for that purpose would be to put ourselves in the same dubious position as the couples we criticise on the grounds that they are 'using' the church. We need to see more clearly that our role is about allowing space for people to encounter the love of God in the way that is possible for them. Weddings are not recruitment drives, or chances to corner people with pressured evangelistic methods. Of course, we would like couples to come to church, and to know the love of God in Christ, but what is happening to them spiritually is between them and God, and, to quote the old hymn, we are 'channels only'. The result of a positive experience of church may be years down the line. A wedding may only be an opportunity for 'pre-evangelism', as someone has called it. It may only be a time for sweeping away misconceptions rather than offering positive insights. But this is God's work, and the timing is God's.

Grasping the opportunity

Every year about 170,000 individuals stand up in a Christian church to declare their commitment. Each wedding is attended by a large number of people who rarely if ever come through church doors at other times. The way we make all these people welcome, and what they see and hear, will have an influence far beyond the wedding day. The church has the responsibility to make the most of this opportunity. We can all do it better. This book simply tries to share ideas that have worked for some. They won't work for everyone, because each place is different. There is no 'right' way to do marriage ministry – but there are certainly some wrong ways, and those are probably rooted in not seeing the huge and positive opportunities that a marriage presents.

2 Selling the product: having confidence in what we do

In this chapter we will look at the task of promoting the church as a venue for weddings. Often we assume that people know their right to get married in church – but the evidence suggests that that is far from being the case.

Dispelling myths

Many couples think they can't have a church wedding because they don't go to church, or haven't been baptized, or are living together. Dispelling these myths and holding out a welcoming hand makes all the difference.

When one of my children was about to be bridesmaid for one of her sisters, she bought a book on how to be a bridesmaid. It was full of what were to my mind preposterous statements, such as that a bridesmaid who became pregnant after being asked should withdraw her acceptance because it would offend the vicar, and that on no account should an off-the-shoulder or low-cut dress be worn because that would offend the vicar and his church. After I had written about this book in my parish magazine, quoting these two examples, a local radio station invited me to talk about it. They also invited the author, who arrived with ample evidence of when and where these things had been said – and said quite recently at that! I was glad I had been given the second slot, so that I could explain that there were eccentrics in every profession, but that the vast majority of clergy wouldn't be offended by either of the issues raised. This underlines one of the problems we are facing: people are quite sure that the church won't allow or will disapprove of this or that. We have to be pro-active in saying that we welcome all couples and would like to support them as they move towards marriage. There are many ways of doing this, some of which are outlined below.

Selling church weddings

Perhaps churches feel that they have enough to cope with in responding to the couples who make an approach to them, and the thought of drumming up more custom seems strange. But for every church that thinks it has enough to cope with, there will be more than one that hasn't reached double figures for weddings for years. 'No one has asked for a wedding here in the last two years,' one vicar said to me. I didn't have the courage to say, 'Have you asked anyone if they would like their wedding in your church?'

It is a large culture shift to move towards selling the idea of a church wedding, but it is one we need to make if the decline in church weddings is to be reversed. Every year since 1992, there have been fewer religious weddings (that is, weddings of all faith communities) in the UK than civil weddings. The decline has been rapid. In 1981, 50.9 per cent of weddings were religious, but in 2004 that figure had fallen to 32.1 per cent. But since the total number of weddings has also fallen, the actual number of religious weddings has gone down from over 179,000 in 1981 to just over 87,000 in 2004. About 84,500 of those were Christian ceremonies.

Improving contact with couples

We should be addressing the need to make contact with our potential wedding couples. There are positive steps we can take on all sorts of levels. Some suggestions that have proved useful are included here.

Wedding fairs

Wedding fairs – curiously, often given an old-fashioned flavour by being called 'fayres' – are very popular. The two days I spent on a stand at a national fair for the launch of *Growing Together* were highly educative. I observed excited brides, even more excited brides' mothers, bored grooms and frightened brides' fathers. I also saw a lot of people making a lot of money out of giving messages about what was 'essential' for a good wedding day. It was a delight to be able to say to people that the church stand was the only one in the entire exhibition that wasn't selling anything – in fact, we were giving things away. If fairs are saying that 'everything you need for your wedding' is to be found there, and the church is totally absent, what message are we giving out?

Meeting the costs

Stands at wedding fairs – even the more local events – are extremely expensive, and we cannot assume that organizers will be willing to give space free, or at reduced rates. If we can work ecumenically, the united voice of all the churches of an area may be a powerful lever to persuade organizers to give us space. Sometimes inviting the bishop, or someone else who will generate publicity for the fair, will persuade organizers to be generous. If we have to pay, then the cost may not be prohibitive if the stand is booked in the name of a diocese, a deanery or a local Churches Together group and every church is willing to chip in. Alternatively, a Christian business with a stand may be willing to carry some church materials as part of its display.

Looking professional

Wedding fairs are full of professionally designed, attractive stands, staffed by well-trained personnel who have huge stocks of glossy literature to give away. How are church groups, who usually have very limited resources, to compete?

Stands It is important to make the stand look as good as possible. A growing number of groups and dioceses have display stands available to borrow (see the Resources section of this book, page 86, for some contact addresses) or your denominational headquarters may be able to put you in touch with people from whom displays can be borrowed. The Archbishops' Council also has a large display available. Sponsorship for such displays has been negotiated in the past, and once created they can be used by others.

'Hand-outs' It's good to have something to give away – experience says that people are unlikely to buy books. The Church House Publishing leaflet *Your marriage in the Church of England* is available at a large discount for those buying in bulk. At some fairs a couple of sugared almonds in a twist of paper or fabric have proved an inexpensive give-away.

Helpers Those staffing the stand need to be well-versed in the kind of questions couples ask. It is likely there will be questions about second marriages, and possibly about blessings of same-sex partnerships.

You may also have to take out some public liability insurance.

Do we feel ourselves above all this commercialism, or do we see the need to be there in the market place? The evidence from those who have run stands at wedding fairs is that great interest is shown. But taking a stand at a fair demands considerable commitment, not only in terms of time, but also of expense. From a start in a local parish, one diocese is developing a 'Think Church Weddings' exhibition to take to wedding fairs. The opportunities are out there for the taking.

DIY wedding exhibitions

It's worth looking at other places where the public go. A local library or museum may have exhibition space for a display such as 'Weddings through the years at St Agatha's'. A display like this would not only be historically interesting, but would also provide a platform to show what happens today. It is amazing to see what wedding memorabilia people have stored away that they are willing to share. Again, if there is not only an exhibition of things, but also a presence of people, the opportunities for sharing the value of the church as a venue begin to open up.

Many churches have used their own premises for exhibitions. As part of their effort to encourage church weddings, one London church displayed dresses and photos for a weekend, and celebrated marriage in the main Sunday service. As a result, they found that in each of the following two years they had more weddings than their total number of weddings for the previous ten years. A rural church in Norfolk regularly puts on an enquiry evening when people can look around the church and discuss, without any obligation, what a church wedding would involve.

Booklets and free literature

In many parts of the country there are commercially produced wedding booklets that advertise the paraphernalia of weddings – cars, florists and the like. That is how this literature is financed. But at least some of these booklets have space within them for articles on various aspects of marriage, and can be a platform for local churches to make clear what they can offer. My experience is that they welcome contributions with open arms.

But with the growth of highly sophisticated software for computers, and increasingly cheap colour laser printing, it is perfectly possible to produce really attractive home-grown literature.

Individual contacts

Church members might be encouraged to suggest to their recently-engaged friends and family that they might like to think about the local church for their wedding. If churches have produced wedding-fair leaflets, as mentioned in the previous paragraph, they could be passed on to engaged couples.

Using the church web site and notice boards

If your church has a web site, it would be useful to include information about getting married in the church, with a contact address for interested couples. It would be wise not to include too many of the rules and regulations, as these can be off-putting and are much better explained face to face.

Similarly, notices on your church notice boards could prompt couples to think about getting married in your church, and tell them who to contact. If the church is kept open, it is good to have leaflets about weddings available for visitors to find.

Improving the product

Think about your local situation, and the buildings you have: what are the selling points that make them or could make them attractive? What makes them less appealing – and is there anything you can do about that? Improvements that apply to weddings apply to other occasions too. Disabled access, good lighting and good sound systems, for example, are important for everyone who comes through our doors for any reason. Often quite small changes can make a big difference to the attractiveness of a building and its surroundings. If we want people to say, 'That looks like a good place for our wedding', then we have to start trying to look at it through their eyes.

3 The church that wants to say Yes: giving a positive message

In this chapter we will explore the way we handle enquiries from couples, and attempt to see how we can lead them positively through the legal minefield that sometimes seems to be lying in front of them. We will also look at some of the other practical issues that can usefully be raised when a wedding is being booked.

First impressions

First impressions matter in all walks of life, so the way we handle preliminary enquiries is going to colour the whole process. 'They didn't seem very interested in us' is not the message we want to convey. The simple word 'Congratulations' spoken to a tentative voice on the phone asking, 'Can we get married in your church?' speaks volumes about being welcoming. If your parish systems demand that wedding bookings are taken at a particular time and place, then at least you have shown personal concern before you go on to say, 'You'll need to come and fill in some forms on a Monday evening.'

The problem is that so often the church seems to say No, even if it wants to say Yes. Of course, we have to work within the laws as they are laid down, and we do no service to anyone by flouting them. But, at least, if you can blame any apparent difficulties on the system, you are keeping yourself on their side as someone who is trying to help them find the way forward. Try comparing these responses, and imagine how they feel to a nervous couple.

'No, you'll have to go to your own parish church.'

'I'm afraid there are all sorts of legal issues we have to comply with – this is the law of the land, not just rules we've got at St Egbert's.'

'Why don't you want to get married in the church in x?'

Getting it right can be difficult. Sometimes couples misunderstand friendly questions as being an interrogation which they need to 'pass' before the marriage can go ahead. So whilst such questions may be splendid, they will come better after the booking is firmly made.

What are the rules?

Residence requirements

The rules at the moment are complex. You can get married in the parish in which either party is resident at the time of the calling of the banns – so in practice that means either place of residence. The problems arise when neither party qualifies in that way. Where that is the case, all is not lost, and there are currently three ways in which a marriage may be possible.

Habitual attendance

If the couple come to church 'habitually' for six months, they can then be entered on the church electoral roll. Once their names are on the church roll, they have the same rights as residents and can therefore get married in the church. What 'habitual' means is not defined, but it is important that there should be consistency of practice within a parish, or there will be food for grievances.

Archbishop's Licence

If there is some strong pastoral reason why a couple should
marry in a church other than their parish church, application
can be made for an Archbishop's Licence. The couple and
the incumbent need to explain why they think it appropriate,
and the opinion of the clergy in their parishes of residence
must be sought.

Superintendent Registrar's Certificate

The couple can obtain a Superintendent Registrar's Certificate.
This also involves residence in the parish, and the rules about
how and when the application may be made are complicated,
and need to be carefully adhered to. Because of that, it is not
an easy option to take.

Qualifying connection

In order to widen the welcome, Synod is now considering
proposals that will give couples a 'qualifying connection'.
The intention is that people who can demonstrate such
a connection will have exactly the same rights as
resident parishioners. If these proposals are accepted, they
may present challenges to popular churches. Not only will
the clergy have to find time for the weddings, but other
people in the church – bell-ringers, organists, choir
members, those who lead marriage preparation courses –
will find that greater demands are made on their time.
Although the proposed qualifications are very broad, it
still won't be open house for weddings. Until these
proposals are accepted, the ways outlined above are the
only ways.

But there's always a way

If a couple really want to marry in a particular church, there are always ways in which they can qualify to do so legally. It is in their power and up to them. So any approach to them that implies they *can't* is dishonest. If we are to be a church that wants to say Yes, then our task is to help them through those legal minefields. But we do need to observe the law.

Second marriages

There will also be those who have a previous partner living from whom they are divorced. The Church now allows second marriages of such people under certain circumstances. There are forms for couples to fill in to help clergy make the decision, which, at the end of the day, is theirs alone, although they can, and in some cases *must*, consult the bishop, or whoever acts on his behalf. All clergy have the right to invoke a conscience clause that stipulates that they are not obliged either to conduct such marriages themselves, or to allow other people to conduct them in churches of which they are the incumbents. There may be policies that PCCs have agreed, but these have no legal force. If a wedding is not possible, then a service of prayer and dedication may be offered if it is felt appropriate.

All this requires great tact and pastoral skill. This is the case whatever the position taken by the priest – whether the response is, 'I am sorry that personally my conscience does not allow me to do this, but can I help you find another way forward?' or, 'I want to be able to say yes, but we have to ensure that your individual circumstances are such that it is the right thing to do.'

It is wise not to take any details of possible dates and times, or fill in the normal forms, until these preliminaries have been dealt with. People respect your taking care to do the right thing, as long as it is done sensitively.

Other restrictions

People will come with other requests that we may or may not be able to meet. They may, for example, want to know if they can marry on Sunday, or Christmas Day, or during Lent.

Marriages are legal any day between 8.00 a.m. and 6.00 p.m. providing they do not interfere with divine service. Any restrictions on days and seasons are by local custom, and not by law. So if for good reasons we are limiting people's choice, again, we need to do so with sensitivity, respecting their legal rights.

Handling bookings

In larger parishes, bookings for weddings may be taken by vergers, parish office staff or administrators. It is important that they should have had a thorough training in the legal stipulations, and also be familiar with the general attitude of the parish, so that they can reflect the same openness. Training can be usefully given from time to time by dioceses and deaneries so that staff from the Diocesan Registry can give authoritative answers to questions.

Filling in forms is a fraught process for most of us, and is particularly difficult for couples not used to churches. Years ago a young woman in her twenties filled in a banns application form for me, and on this form she wrote down that she was a widow. (On the forms we then used, the word had to be written in.) It was perfectly possible that this was her second marriage, and her first husband had died as a young man, and as her wedding was taking place elsewhere, it seemed unnecessary and insensitive to make enquiries. She was present when we called the banns, and afterwards asked why I had said she was a widow, when she wasn't. We consulted the form she had filled in, and there it was – a dreadful example of what nerves can do to people faced with formal pieces of paper.

All of us will occasionally meet with someone who can't read and/or write. Offering to fill in the form for them can avoid great embarrassment.

One church ensures that there is a waiting area, equipped with albums of photographs of previous weddings in the church and wedding magazines, where the couple can wait if the 'wedding bookers' are busy. Those doing the bookings are members of the congregation, and act as a link with the church. They work in twos and as well as filling in the forms are encouraged to chat with the couple. Because a good number of people are involved, each pair of 'bookers' works with a limited number of couples. All this has been so positive that some couples have invited their 'bookers' to their wedding.

Information packs

This is the time for making sure that people know all the local customs, and understand how everything will now progress. An information pack is tremendously helpful because it can be referred to as the months go on. These packs vary enormously. Some are quite excellent and clear guides, attractively presented, and this makes all the difference to those important first impressions.

It is useful to cover the following areas.

Legal issues

Legal issues include dates for banns; the need to get them called in any other parish of residence; and details of how to go about applying for an Archbishop's Licence or Superintendent Registrar's Certificate.

Forms of service

Many parishes provide a copy of the *Common Worship* marriage booklet, or their locally produced version of the wedding service. It is good to remind people of their opportunity to have the BCP or Series 1 services.

Choices within the service

The range of choice will vary according to local custom. The wider the choice, the more involved the couple will feel. An example of how the choices can be given to couples is to be found in Appendix 2. You may wish to draw their attention to:

Holy Communion

If the couple are communicants, the possibility of receiving communion at the wedding needs to be explained.

Readings

In the *Common Worship* booklet, the suggested readings are written out in full. Some parishes provide their own sheet of readings, either written in full, or as biblical references, and some also make suggestions for additional non-biblical readings, or give details of web sites where readings for weddings can be found. Any non-biblical readings need to be approved before they are included.

Hymns

Indicate how many hymns the couple may have, and where they come in the service. It is sensible to retain the right to suggest the order in which they come, so that the words may fit as appropriately as possible. Some parishes have created a hymn booklet of popular hymns for weddings, either the full texts or their first lines, to help couples choose.

Encouraging people to choose well-known hymns is always advisable. A good starting point is to ask if the couple themselves know the hymn they are considering. If one of them doesn't know it, then neither will many others who will be at the wedding! There are lots of web sites that offer lists (see page 87 for some web site addresses).

Music

The local options need to be outlined:

- whether there is a choir (with suggestions of what they could sing);
- whether there is a music group;
- how to get in touch with the organist;
- whether CDs can be used;
- the procedure if friends are to be invited to sing or play.

Recordings

If anyone is going to make a video or audio recording, local rules about where they can position themselves should be explained. Similarly, couples will need to know what photography (both professional and amateur) is permitted. A licence is required for copyright material, and organists are entitled to an additional fee if a recording is made, even if it is on a relative's camcorder.

Flowers

Churches have a variety of systems for flowers at weddings, and it is useful for couples to know from the outset about the system that is followed at the church where they will be married, and also about any charges.

Bells

If the church has bells, include information about how they are booked, and whether they are rung both before and after the service or just afterwards.

Confetti

The local rules about what may and may not be thrown can be set out so that the couple can include this information with their invitation details.

Car parking

Many churches have very limited car parking space. A guide, possibly with a local map, explaining where guests might most conveniently park is useful. These days it is helpful to give the postcode of the church for those using sat-nav equipment in their cars.

Fees

More often than not an information pack can only give a guide figure because the fees are usually increased from January each year. It is useful to say how and when fees should be paid. I know of one parish that issues a pro forma sheet listing all the fees, distinguishing between the statutory fees that *must* be paid, and additional payments that may be requested (for example, for the organist, bells and flowers). This form also gives the couple the opportunity to make a gift-aided donation over and above the fees on the basis that the church fees in total will still be the smallest bill of the day. A gift aid form is included. (*Note* the fees themselves cannot be gift-aided.)

Schedule

Some churches also include a check-list of what needs to be done during the countdown to the day – three months before, one month before, and so on. (See also the suggestions on 'information evenings' on pages 10 and 32.)

4 Towards the marriage: marriage preparation and wedding preparation

We need to distinguish between marriage preparation and wedding preparation. Both are important, and need to be given thoughtful planning. This chapter is about how churches can help couples prepare for married life by taking part in some form of marriage preparation course, and outlines some of the issues involved in setting up such courses. The following chapter will look at preparing for the wedding day.

A variety of ways

There is a huge variety of approaches to marriage preparation, or marriage exploration, as some of us would prefer to call it. Some parishes provide courses for individual couples, others for groups, and yet others have a combination of the two. The only piece of academic research was conducted by the University of Surrey, working with data from churches of all denominations in the south ('Church Support of Marriage and Adult Relationships in Southern England', UNIS Roehampton, 2003). It showed that couples did not mind which approach was followed. Marriage courses were appreciated greatly by the vast majority, whatever form they took. We should take this as great encouragement.

The rate of uptake of courses in different parishes probably bears some relationship to the confidence with which we offer them. If we believe we have something good to offer, and assume people will take it up, we are likely to have a better response than if we tentatively suggest that they might like to come to something which some people have sometimes found useful. In many parishes, it's taken for granted that booking such a course is a normal and right part of making arrangements for a wedding.

Who does it?

The answer seems to be either the clergy, or a lay team, or outsiders brought in for the purpose. Clergy will always want to be involved in the *wedding* preparation, but there is no reason why they should be the appropriate people to do *marriage* preparation. If the preparation offered is anything beyond a single day, it will be hugely demanding on their time. There are some priests (and I include myself here) who think that this is a right use of their time and skills. But in any parish there may be others who are, or who could become, suitably qualified.

Some dioceses provide training for pastoral assistants. If parishes are using the Foccus Marriage Inventory (where couples fill in an extensive questionnaire, which is then analysed by an expert, and the results fed back), they will be trained to use it. Holy Trinity Brompton offers training for people using their marriage course. Relate may be able to provide personnel to run marriage preparation courses. But of course employing outside agencies will always have cost implications.

A parish in Lancashire that has developed a strong pattern of marriage ministry makes the valid point that couples are much more likely to be drawn into a sense of belonging if they make relationships with lay people in the church. Couples may also be more open with people who are not authority figures in their minds. Pastoral care is the responsibility of the whole community, not just the clergy. As has been wisely said: 'People need to be "known" not processed.'

Co-operation between churches

With many couples getting married at some distance from where they live or work – a situation that is likely to get more and more common when residence becomes less likely as a qualification for marriage in a particular church – then we have to look to how we can co-operate to help each other right across the country and beyond. It ought to be possible to set up a system whereby couples can receive suitable preparation near where they live. Putting people in touch is the hard part – and this is where networks like FLAME and the Mothers' Union can be invaluable. It ought to be possible to set up a system whereby a couple is put in touch with a diocesan contact, who will then link them up with a parish or deanery where they can take a marriage preparation course.

The preparation for the wedding itself will need to be done in the church where the wedding is to take place – but simply separating the two aspects may be a positive step. This style of co-operation may also be useful on a local level, where small churches have only a few weddings, and want to share the marriage aspect of preparation with their neighbours across a deanery or within an ecumenical grouping. If we don't start asking for such co-operation, it will never happen.

Some overseas dioceses demand participation in some kind of preparation scheme, and a couple living in this country have to find someone who will provide it prior to their marriage abroad. We ought to be making their task easier. It works the other way, too: a Canadian couple who, because of family connections, were able to get an Archbishop's Licence to marry in my parish were obviously unable to take part in any preparation I provided. When I asked them to find someone in Ontario to take them on, they had no problem, and very much valued the experience. The priest concerned subsequently wrote to me saying how much he had enjoyed working with them.

When might marriage preparation take place?

Working with individual couples

Working with individual couples allows for flexibility, the number and length of the sessions being by mutual agreement. Another advantage is that the couple have the freedom to bring up personal issues that may need some time to explore – not necessarily with the person doing the preparation. Talking about 'till death do us part', for example, may raise some issues about bereavement and grief that haven't been worked through and are more pressing than the forthcoming marriage. I can think of couples who have needed to address problems about alcohol dependence, or sexual abuse with someone suitably qualified. The marriage preparation session may be the only place where a couple feel safe enough to raise delicate matters. Someone who is not simply delivering a set course is free to go down whatever avenues are appropriate. This is pastoral care in its widest and deepest sense. I have even been asked to meet with parents who are getting in the way of the couple's relationship. And a FLAME officer in a Midlands diocese found there was a market for courses for parents whose children were getting married.

Working with a group of couples

Many parishes choose to work with small groups, either fitting everything into a single meeting, or arranging a series of meetings. This is less demanding on time but is problematic for couples who, for unavoidable reasons, cannot manage that particular date. Group work has the advantage of being potentially less intrusive, so a shy couple might feel that it is easier to handle. A further advantage is that people spark one another. A great deal of peer learning takes place within a group.

Parishes that run a one-off event for each new group have interesting approaches:

Some arrange a Sunday activity. The couples all attend a morning service, are provided with lunch and tea, and may end with a short evening service.

Others have a Saturday event, either half a day, or a full day. Because wedding-day arrangements are often also being covered, there is limited scope for looking at relationship issues.

In some parishes, a weekend is given over to marriage preparation. This allows more freedom to look at a wider range of topics.

What topics might be covered?

A generation or two ago marriage preparation courses included sessions led by people from outside the church – a doctor to talk about sex, a banker to talk about finance and a solicitor to talk about buying houses, for example. These days the majority of couples are already living together, have joint accounts and their own flat or house. They may already have children. We need to address the real issues that concern today's couples, so questions about infertility, step-parenting, coping with former partners and aging parents might come higher on the agenda.

If you ask any group what topics to include, you'll find that there is enough material for a weekly session for a year. So some prioritizing is essential. If people are using off-the-peg courses, that will be done for them, but most courses have weaknesses as well as strengths, and there is a lot to be said for mixing and matching to suit your particular context. Some parishes have done this – one has even rounded up its amateur dramatics buffs and made its own videos.

Courses come and go, and no one size fits all. However, if a course does not cover the Big C's – Commitment, Communication and Conflict then it is not going to be valuable.

Who pays?

Even home-grown courses will have costs. The majority of churches want to offer marriage preparation without making a charge, but that is not always possible. These days, however, there seems little or no resistance to paying for what you get – particularly if it is a quality product. It seems reasonable, therefore, to charge an 'administration fee' to cover expenses – costs incurred producing a workbook, or the fee for processing a Foccus inventory, for example.

Growing Together

Because there is never time to cover all the topics we might wish, it is useful to be able to back up what is provided with some material that a couple can work through on their own. This is the thinking behind my own book *Growing Together* (see page 85) which takes 13 topics, and with each one asks couples to tackle questions: 'Where are we coming from?', 'Where are we now?' and 'Where are we going?' Parishes are increasingly giving this book to supplement their preparation, while some have found ways to produce their own material, using this book as a guide. A book suggesting ways in which *Growing Together* can be used for day, weekend and on-going courses is scheduled for publication in autumn 2007.

5 Towards the wedding: practical issues

This chapter covers preparing for the wedding day itself, from the first contact up to the rehearsal.

Marking the decision to marry

Booking the wedding is a private event, but many churches then have a public acknowledgement of the couple's intentions. Some churches give a present, possibly a Bible, or a book about marriage such as *Pocket Prayers for Marriage* (Church House Publishing, 2004) or *Growing Together* (Church House Publishing, 2005). If you have someone in the congregation whose hobby is calligraphy, you can add a personal touch. My own church, in addition to a Bible, gives a tea towel with pictures of the church on it.

One church, in need of new kneelers, encourages couples to find someone in their family who will make a kneeler embroidered with the couple's initials. This can be used at the wedding and then added to the parish stock as a record of the service. If there are people with needlework skills in the parish, they might be willing to make kneelers as a service to couples. It could prove a delight in later years to find the couples bringing their children to hunt for 'Mummy and Daddy's kneeler'.

A more unusual and formal public expression of being on the journey towards a marriage has been developed by a parish in Sussex, where every couple is offered the option of a betrothal ceremony. This ceremony, which takes place at the time of the first reading of the banns, includes a formal statement of intention and the blessing of the engagement ring. It adds a positive note to what is otherwise a rather negative moment – 'If there is any just cause or impediment why these persons may not be joined together in holy matrimony . . .' You can read about this in detail, and the rationale behind it, in the essay, 'The Case for Betrothal', by Reg Harcus in the useful compendium of papers *Celebrating Christian Marriage*, edited by Adrian Thatcher (T & T Clark, 2001).

Getting alongside

Where people are attending a church in order to have their names put on the electoral roll, the opportunities to befriend them are endless. The part this has to play in the mission of the church can't be overstated. A couple who came to our church for this reason, having never been churchgoers before, didn't appear again after the wedding. We thought that maybe it was an instance of our being 'used'. But a few months later we received a letter from them explaining that immediately after the wedding the husband had got a new job in a different area, and that they had made contact with and settled into their new church. They wrote to thank the congregation for making them so welcome and for the part they had played in their journey of faith.

Some churches take photographs of the couple and put them on a notice board with the date of the wedding and an encouragement to people to pray regularly for them. Other churches have a lay 'sponsor' for each couple. The sponsor gets to know them, attends on the wedding day, and is responsible for sending anniversary cards afterwards. One parish has developed this into a much more extensive 'Cana ministry' in which couples are befriended in all sorts of practical and spiritual ways. All these suggestions help the whole congregation to feel that the marriages are not private events, but occasions they are all involved in and care about.

One Mothers' Union branch sends the couple a card in the week prior to the wedding that simply says they are being prayed for as their day approaches. Other churches pray for the couple by name on the Sundays before and after the wedding. *Common Worship* has 'Prayers at the Calling of the Banns', which can be used. Another church rings the bride and groom's homes on the day of the wedding just to reassure them that everything is ready. Taking care of the couple in these and other ways is part of the gospel of love we attempt to model.

Preparing for the wedding day

Information evenings

Many of the decisions couples will need to make will have been raised for them if they are given an information pack as described in Chapter 3. Some churches provide an information evening, when all the people who will be involved – the organist, flower-arrangers, vergers, and so on – can speak, and be on hand for questions and consultation. There will, however, always be people who can't manage the time arranged for these information evenings so we need to let them know how to contact the relevant people individually.

Some churches turn these information evenings into social occasions by beginning with refreshments, or even a meal. In large parishes with many weddings, it helps to run such evenings twice or three times in the year. From the church's perspective, details such as flowers and music may seem relatively unimportant, but they may loom very large in the eyes of some members of families.

Flowers

There probably need to be parish policies about what happens about flowers on days when there is more than one wedding. Can the couples come to an agreement about the flowers they would like to have, and sharing costs? Is it possible to change the flowers between weddings? What guidance can be offered to outside professionals?

I recall with horror arriving one evening for a wedding rehearsal, and going with the verger into what I thought was an empty church, to find that we could not see the altar for the hugely over-sized arrangements in the chancel and sanctuary. It was only after I had said to him, 'Isn't that awful?' that I noticed the bride's mother sitting in a side aisle. We learned from that to give outside arrangers information about the maximum dimensions for their handiwork.

Music

Music also needs to be thought about at a local level. These days there are lots of CDs available with ideas for voluntaries. But not every parish church has an organist capable of tackling the Widor 'Toccata', and not every organ is suitable for grandiose pieces – on a tiny village organ the Widor might sound like a symphony being played on recorders. It is great if circumstances allow total freedom of choice, but in churches where the organist's skills are limited, it is much better to follow the recommendation of the Royal School of Church Music and offer couples a list of what the organist can play.

Even when well-known hymns are chosen, we need to check that the tune is the one the couple are expecting. Quite apart from those hymns that have 'old' and 'new' tunes, there are others that have two equally known and loved 'old' tunes. 'Love divine all loves excelling' is the obvious example – Stainer's tune 'Love divine' and the Welsh tune 'Blaenwern' are both popular. But one is a four-line tune, and the other eight lines. The couple need to decide which tune they would like to have, not only for the organist, but also for the printer, if an order of service is being printed.

Orders of service

Helping couples make their choices

Common Worship allows a great deal of choice – although not all churches tell couples that! Setting out clearly what choices are available, and getting clear decisions, can be made simpler by using a form that the couple can work through in their own time and consult the clergy about as issues arise. In Appendix 2 you will find an example of such a sheet, which would need to be adapted to local situations.

Printing

Getting orders of service printed correctly can be a minefield, particularly if we encourage couples to make their own choices out of the many available. If professional printers are being used, it is wise to suggest that the church, as well as the couple, checks the proofs. In an article in the *Church Times*, Canon David Winter referred to an order of service that included all the vows, but unfortunately read, 'To hate and to hold from this day forward'.

Many churches these days have access to sophisticated printing facilities, either in their own, or in a neighbour's church. By offering to produce the order of service 'in-house', you can be sure of what is included. *Common Worship* has an excellent 'Pastoral Introduction', which, it says, 'may be read by those present before the service begins'. But if you are not using the *Common Worship* wedding booklets, those present can only read it if it is included on the printed order.

Some churches have a brief history of their building that they also include when printing an order of service, and many provide a selection of pictures for possible use on the front.

Some churches provide a commentary on what is happening, so that, for example, under the heading 'The Declarations' an explanation reads, 'The Minister asks the congregation and the couple if they know any legal impediment to the marriage, and then asks the couple to make their declaration of intent.' An example of how that can be done can be found in Appendix 1.

The liturgy pages to be found on the Church of England web site (www.cofe.anglican.org/worship/liturgy/commonworship/texts/marriage/marriagefront.html) or in *Visual Liturgy* (Church House Publishing) make compiling a tailor-made order of service very easy for any computer user. Some churches will either print the order of service themselves, or will provide an electronic copy for couples who wish to use their own printer. Either way, the chances are that we are offering a considerable financial saving, and are ensuring that what is provided is exactly what is wanted and needed. It can also generate some income for the church.

The rehearsal

Most churches offer a rehearsal in church. This enables everyone to see how things feel on the ground, and to iron out any little details that may be worrying those taking part.

Timing

Wherever possible, the rehearsal needs to be very close to the event – often this is the only way the majority of participants can be there. A last-minute rehearsal also has the advantage of keeping things fresh in everyone's mind.

Who should come?

The rule of thumb is that anyone who has anything to do should be there – so in addition to the bride and groom, you need the best man, bridesmaids, parents, lesson readers and ushers. Bringing everybody together may remind couples of small points that had been overlooked in the pressure of so many other things. Many brides, for example, realize that they haven't decided which bridesmaids are to walk together. And if very young children are involved, it may become apparent that contingency plans are needed in case they 'throw a wobbly' on the day.

I recall a wonderful wedding where there were to be eight under-fives as bridesmaids. At the rehearsal we decided that the only way to marshal them was to put out a 'magic carpet' on which they would all sit. What might have been chaotic became something easily understood and simple. That same rehearsal also showed the value of checking details. The family were Russian émigrés, and had chosen the Imperial Russian Anthem for the entrance of the bride. The music was to be played by a military brass group. Fortunately the bandmaster came to the rehearsal, and when I hummed 'God the all-terrible' as we walked down the aisle, he said, 'But that isn't what we've prepared.' Having been asked for 'the old Russian national anthem', he was ready with, not the current one, but the Communist anthem. The effect of that on the family would have been indescribable.

Movements

The rehearsal provides an opportunity to work out who is sitting where, and how everyone will know when to move.

The groom and best man need to make a policy decision about whether they will turn and watch the bride's arrival, or stay looking forward until she arrives alongside. If they each choose differently, it can look as if one of them isn't interested and the other is.

Kneeling is not something most couples are used to doing, and it is worth rehearsing how to get up and down with dignity. I remember as a curate marrying a market trader from Iran, whose English was negligible. As a result, the rehearsal was getting quite lengthy, and the bride offered to explain everything to him later. So we didn't practise kneeling. On the day he knelt according to his national custom, sitting bent-legged on the floor. She, fortunately, was wearing a dress that allowed her to do the same, but they were so far down that putting my stole round their hands from the top of three steps brought me near to strangulation.

So it really is worth going through all the actions of the service, from the bride's entrance through to getting the procession in place for going out. If you feel strongly about couples saving the full vows for the day itself, just saying a line or two to get the volume right is a practical compromise.

Readers

Rehearsing readers enables you to ensure they are clearly heard, and mispronunciations are picked up. Some churches insist that readers who have been unable to come to the rehearsal arrive early on the day of the wedding to practise in the church.

Vergers

The rehearsal also gives the verger, or whoever looks after the church building and furnishings, the opportunity to check practical details such as how many seats are to be reserved, and whether wheelchairs will need to be accommodated. I recall thinking on one occasion that the verger was being over-fussy, but was firmly put in my place after the wedding by a letter from the couple that said how confident they had felt when they heard his questions because they saw that everything was being arranged so carefully and with such attention to detail.

Orders of service

When the printing has been organized by the couple rather than the church, some churches ask for the orders of service to be brought to the rehearsal so that there is no risk of their not being available for the earliest arrivals on the day. After having had to delay the start of one wedding whilst someone went to get them from under the hall table at the bride's house, that is something I always do now!

6 The day itself: making things run smoothly

This chapter looks at what happens at the wedding from the perspective of the congregation and the church as a whole. It is about how we can provide a warm welcome. Chapter 7 looks at things from the point of view of the person conducting the wedding.

A calm and welcoming atmosphere

Those who are trying to get things organized – ushers, for instance – are often ill at ease because they don't know the building. It is important that whoever is looking after the wedding on behalf of the church should be there in very good time to encourage them and show them what they need to know. If hymn books or service books are to be given out, they need to be at hand. A warm atmosphere, both literally and in terms of friendliness, sets the right tone.

The organist is being paid, so it is reasonable to expect there to be background organ music for a while before the service – again, this helps create the right atmosphere.

Arrival at the church

Many reception venues have a board outside saying that they welcome the families of X and Y. A similar notice outside the church flags up that this is an occasion that we value and not 'just another wedding'. It also helps those who are not certain that they have found the right church. A friend of mine very much enjoyed a wedding he went to a few years ago – unfortunately, it wasn't the one he had intended to be at!

One church with a talented banner group constructed a beautiful three-dimensional banner made up largely of artificial flowers. That in itself was a wonderful decoration for the church. But what made it particularly appreciated was that silk letters of the couple's initials were tacked on to it.

Creature comforts

Most of the congregation will have travelled some distance on the day of the wedding, so churches that have obvious directions to their toilets are being really helpful, particularly to parents with children. Most people don't like to ask – not least, in case there isn't one! One church that has no hostelries or cafés nearby opens up their church hall for coffee an hour before the service – a great welcome for those who have come a distance. Some churches offer a crèche during part or all of the service. Others ensure that there are books and quiet toys for children.

Notices

In many churches notices are given out before the bride arrives. Though we may have the greatest desire in the world to be positive, inevitably some announcements are going to be 'thou shalt nots' – and these especially shouldn't be part of the wedding itself. It is important, for example, to ask people to switch off their mobiles, and to tell them about what is permitted in terms of photography and confetti. A vicar in West Yorkshire invites people to donate £5 to a charity of their choice if their phone goes off during the service.

But these negative remarks can be counterbalanced by delight at seeing everyone, and advice that there is someone at the back of church should any help be needed. Everyone can also be encouraged to join in both sung and spoken parts of the service as part of their gift of love to the couple. Some people like to rehearse the congregation in their response to the question about supporting the couple – and that is particularly relevant if these words are not on the printed order of service.

Given out a few minutes before the service, notices help settle the noise. They can then conclude with the suggestion that the 'Pastoral Introduction' be quietly read as everyone waits for the bride (see page 34).

All this can help create an atmosphere of welcome, expectancy and reverence as the bride arrives.

The wedding service

Clear signals to the organist that it is time to start the music for the bride's entry are important. The church where I learned the organ as a teenager had a verger who sidled down the south aisle to the organist very solemnly and discreetly, and then, being very deaf, bawled at the top of his voice: 'They're ready now, Mr Verney.' That *didn't* help create the right tone!

As we have seen, some of the churches who produce their own order of service like to add a practical commentary to help people understand what is happening (see page 35). Appendix 1 suggests one way that can be done. This is another example of how we can gently take a congregation by the hand, and help them to get the most out of what is happening. A written explanation is preferable to a spoken commentary – the more words we add to the fine words of the liturgy, the less those words stand out.

After the service

Bearing in mind that couples are not going to be taking it in, one church produces an A4 sheet with the sermon printed in full and a colour picture of the church. That is put into a plastic folder together with the marriage certificate. Another church, similarly, gives a good quality picture of the church, headed with the date and time of the wedding, in a folder tied with ribbon. Yet another gives an inscribed Bible from which the lesson has been read. In at least one case, that simple act led to a couple reading more, and finding real faith for the first time.

So, hopefully, both bridal party and congregation will have felt welcomed and taken seriously. They will have been enabled to join in and to enjoy taking part. Then they leave – and even that can be done in helpful ways. Often couples are kept in the porch by photographers, and the congregation is left queuing for ages behind them. If you have more than one door, you might consider following the example of the church that siphons off the rest of the congregation through another door so that they can go round and also take photos of the couple in the church doorway. It isn't very welcoming for someone to be standing at the back after the service jangling a bunch of keys in an ostentatious way!

One church tells of the local custom of tying the church gates at weddings. Village children allow the couple out only when coins have been handed to them. This is part of their community life, and means the clergy literally have a captive audience with whom to share the joy of the day outside the church as well as in it.

7 Doing the service well: 'The service was wonderful, Vicar!'

The words 'grandmother', 'suck' and 'eggs' float into my mind as I write this chapter. Clergy rightly have different styles and ways of leading services. What is offered here are Aunt Sally ideas about conducting weddings, ideas with which my colleagues are very welcome to disagree. But to the increasing numbers of younger clergy who have had little opportunity to learn to take weddings, I offer these suggestions as ideas to think about, while more experienced priests may be able to use them as a way of refreshing their practice.

Liturgy as mission

One of the glories of the Church of England is its genius for liturgy. There are those, of course, who say that liturgy died with Thomas Cranmer, but in fact we are the beneficiaries of generations of scholars and practitioners who have honed the words and actions of marriage rites to meet the needs of a changing society.

Underlying aims

It is quite a healthy exercise to write down the words you would like to hear about a wedding. I will start the list off with 'joyful', 'dignified' and 'accessible' – but maybe you would have more to add. There is an old joke about the difference between a priest and an actor. It says that an actor is someone who speaks fiction as if it were truth, and a priest is someone who speaks truth as if it were fiction. At a wedding, we priests have the script, the form of the liturgical text, but whether or not we communicate the truth will depend on how we deliver the lines. Our delivery is what will make the truth 'accessible'.

Tone

My first two words – 'joyful' and 'dignified' – need to be held in tension. It is lovely to have laughter at a wedding, and there will be times, maybe in the notices beforehand, or during the sermon, when humour can be very productive, helping people to relax and think. But it can be overdone and needs to be held in balance with an element of dignity. A couple told me about a wedding they had recently attended that had been taken by a priest who, they said, really ought to be a stand-up comedian. They had been very impressed with his skills. But as the wedding went on, it became clear that he was going over the top, and the end result was that they came away feeling that they had been at a performance, not a service. When, for example, he came to the words, 'all that I have I share with you', he added, 'and that includes the sports car, John.' Laughter from congregation, but total breakdown in the rhythm and dignity of the moment.

On the other hand, taking the old name for the service 'The Solemnization of Matrimony' too literally will result in overbalance in the opposite direction. Maybe it would help us all to meditate on Ecclesiastes 3.1-8: 'For everything there is a season, and a time for every matter under heaven.'

Vesture

Churchmanship and local custom will dictate what is worn. Whatever it is, it ought to look good – everyone else will be wearing 'best bib and tucker', whether that be morning dress or clean jeans. If you are wearing a stole, it is worth looking to acquiring one of the very beautiful white stoles with symbols of weddings on them. These are now easily available. Wearing a cope, if your church has one, can be the ecclesiastical equivalent of suits and posh frocks. It says something about this being a special moment.

Taking the congregation by the hand

Congregations like to know what they are doing, and the wedding will begin much more positively if, just before the entry music starts, you ask everyone to stand. Otherwise, and especially when the music is less familiar, some will not be aware that this is the moment of the bride's entrance, and there will be confusion as some stand and others later realize they should have done so.

Clergy differ on what to announce as the service progresses, and it is certainly possible to say too much. But given that usually the majority of the congregation are not regular churchgoers, it is courteous to help them to do the expected thing. If, for example, what you mean by 'Let us pray' is 'Let us kneel and pray', then it is better to say it – or, preferably, to say, 'Let us sit or kneel', so that people with troublesome knees are not embarrassed if they are unable to comply.

Although *Common Worship* makes suggestions about the posture of the couple – 'The couple stand before the minister', 'The husband and wife kneel' – there are no equivalent instructions for the congregation. So, again, it is part of making people feel comfortable, to explain what they are expected to do. If they see the couple kneel for the 'Blessing of the Marriage', as the rubric suggests, they may feel they should do the same. But there is a great sense of solemnity at that moment if everyone else in church is standing. So prefacing the Blessing with the instruction, 'The congregation remains standing as we ask for God's blessing on N and N', and then whispering a reminder to the couple, '. . . and you kneel' ensures that everyone knows where they are. Some churches have special wedding kneelers. Avoid the mistake of one parish dedicated to St Mary the Virgin, where one kneeler was embroidered with 'St Mary' and the other with 'The Virgin'!

Let's take it from the top . . .

Coming in

Opinions differ about whether the priest should lead the bride in, or wait at the chancel for her arrival. The advantage of leading her in is that she can be welcomed and reassured that everything is as planned and the bridal party can be checked to see if they are all ready. Another advantage is that the speed of the walk down the aisle can be controlled. Most people find it hard to walk very slowly at this point, and tend to be quite speedy. In all but the largest churches, that results in not hearing much of the chosen music. The congregation want to see the bride, not the vicar, so it is sense to leave a longish gap between them. The vicar then simply acts as a pacemaker.

Other clergy feel they are better waiting at the chancel step to welcome the bride and groom on behalf of the church. Some greet the bride at the door, and then walk to the front before asking everyone to stand for her formal entrance.

The option is there for a couple to come in together, and that may be their wish. Where they have been living together for a length of time, and especially if the bride does not have the choice of coming in with her father (or mother), to enter together can be most appropriate. Alternatively, the bride can enter without a 'supporter'. As with so many aspects of the *Common Worship* service, allowing the couple to make the choices for themselves, as far as the building permits, is highly desirable. It is their day, not ours. Appendix 2 has an example of a form that may be given to a couple to help them make these choices, but it will need adaptation to suit individual parishes (see pages 19–21 and 74–79).

If there is to be a choir, it is usually best if they are in their place five minutes before the service so that their arrival is not mixed up with the entrance of the bride.

Getting organized

Careful rehearsal can ensure that the entry music that has been requested is, on the one hand, long enough to cover all the actions that need to happen – the arrival of the bride at the chancel step, her disposal of flowers to a bridesmaid and equipping the bridal party with their service sheets or hymnbooks – and, on the other hand, is heard to the end. Some music doesn't lend itself to be shortened.

It is better to start the procession after the music has been playing for a minute or so than to be standing at the front waiting for it to finish.

If the bride is wearing a veil over her face, this is a good time to have a bridesmaid help her turn it back so that everything is ready for the service to flow smoothly once the music stops.

The Introduction

There is freedom to welcome people informally rather than using the 'grace' provided. But if there has already been a welcome in the context of earlier notices, a second welcome is probably an unnecessary duplication.

The sentence from 1 John and the prayer are optional, and although the text indicates that everyone will say the prayer (in this way ensuring that the congregation are positively involved from the beginning), there may be occasions when it is pastorally more sensitive if it is said by the priest alone.

The Preface

The couple may choose which of the two alternative Prefaces they prefer. The main text offers the opportunity to omit the reference to the birth of children, which may be significant if the couple are past child-bearing years, or know they will not be able to have a family.

Although the couple will no doubt have been referred to by name at the Notices, or in the Greeting, this is the first place where names are used formally. It is up to the couple to say how they are to be addressed. Here, they may want 'informal' names – Dave and Sue – or even nicknames. At the Declarations, however, and especially at the Vows, the solemnity of what they are doing requires the use of their formal names, but not necessarily all of them. I recall a 'bruiser' I married being much relieved that his friends would not need to find out that his middle name was Shirley.

The Preface is set out in paragraphs, which is a hint to us to break up what is quite a long speech. If the priest knows it well enough, it will be possible to look at the congregation during the reading of the Preface, which, again, draws them into the action of the service. Some churches get the bridal party to sit down at this point, providing chairs to one side for the bride and groom. That has the advantage of allowing everyone to relax a little, and focus on the words being said.

The Declarations

Although *Common Worship* allows for Declarations and Vows to be made one after the other, as in previous orders of service, the main text suggests the more logical order of declaring intent, reflecting on that by means of the readings and sermon, and then proceeding to the Vows. If only the couple, and not the congregation as well, stand for this part of the service, even greater solemnity is given to the Vows when everyone is then invited to stand.

It may seem a small point, but to speak less loudly when saying the words addressed to the couple, makes what is said feel more personal.

If the couple have chosen the 'thee/thou' forms for the Vows, there is a good argument for substituting the equivalent 1662/Series 1 thee/thou questions at the Declarations, so that the two most formal bits of the service are of a piece.

The Collect

Inviting people to pray sounds easy – but if the congregation are standing at this point, they may interpret it as an instruction to kneel. The rubric says that silence is kept. Most people, including regular churchgoers, are not used to silence. It is therefore helpful to preface the Collect with a very brief explanation. So, for example, we might say, 'As we stand [sit] let us bring our own prayers for John and Jane to God and ask his blessing on them. After a short silence, I will offer all our thoughts to God in a prayer.'

Silence can have its dangers. Once after I had asked people to pray silently for the couple, and was standing with my eyes closed, a piping three-year-old voice said, 'He's gone to sleep!'

The Readings

This is a good moment for the couple (and anyone else who may be standing) to sit down. They will get much more from listening to the readings and sermon if they are more relaxed, and less on show. The couple will hopefully have chosen their readings carefully. The readers will hopefully have been rehearsed.

It is worth thinking about how the readers will get to the place from which they will read. If there are two readings, having one person come, read and return, followed by someone else walking out to read, can spoil the flow of the service. It works better if both come out together, and take it in turns to go to the lectern, or wherever they will read from, and then return to their seats together.

Sometimes couples are keen to have several readings. Whilst it is good to keep the logic of a 'Ministry of the Word', it can be helpful to move one, particularly if it's a non-biblical reading, to another point. After the Blessing of the Marriage and before the Registration is possibly a good moment, but it really depends on the nature of the reading.

The Sermon

The place where we *are* invited to add words to the liturgy is in the sermon. Here is a golden opportunity to tell people something of the love of God at a time when 'love is in the air'. I once did a survey to find out how many people remembered what had been said in the sermon on their wedding day. Not surprisingly, the majority couldn't remember very much at all. They were rightly full of their own thoughts. So the sermon is probably more properly directed at the congregation. Sadly, some clergy have a wedding sermon – or even two! – that they trot out time after time. In small communities it is not only the organist and choir who know the sermon off by heart.

On an occasion such as this, we are talking about a two- or three-minute homily. It isn't hard to make it relate to the couple. To pick up their choice of reading and say, 'John and Jane chose that passage from . . .' is much warmer than to announce, 'As we heard in the reading . . .' Maybe you can refer to their work, or their hobbies. Anything like this honours the uniqueness of the occasion, and says to everyone that you care about this couple as two special people.

Occasionally you can risk going over the top! On one occasion, I heard that a bridegroom-to-be, when asked if they would be having communion at the wedding, as another family member had done, replied that he didn't like wine, so it would have to be beer, and you needed popcorn to go with that. He wasn't being irreverent, although I realize it can look like that on paper. I decided to rise to the occasion, and at the sermon produced a can of 4X beer, and talked about X as a sign of love, and the four words for love in the New Testament. The couple and I then shared a brief tipple! I showed some uncooked and then some fluffy cooked popcorn, and talked about how love can transform us, and the bowl of popcorn was passed around the congregation while the registers were signed.

Another time, the couple had chosen Auden's poem 'O tell me the truth about love' as an additional reading. But they told me they were altering what is arguably the best line. Instead of:

> *When it comes, will it come without warning,*
> *Just as I'm picking my nose?*

they wanted, 'just as I'm picking a rose'. I warned them that Auden would turn in his grave, and I would have to tell everyone. They went along with that – so I was able to talk about how we can think of marriage in a romantic way, or in a down-to-earth way, and how there is room for both.

Erring on the side of brevity is always right. The theatrical precept of 'leave them wanting more' is much the best way. We all know the story of the child who said she preferred the curate's sermons to the vicar's because the curate said, 'Finally . . .' and finished, whereas the vicar said, 'Lastly . . .' and lasted.

The Vows

We need to flag up the solemnity of this central moment of the service. Many churches therefore ask all the bridal party to stand. The decision about where bridesmaids are to stand is significant here. If they are behind the bride, the congregation's view will be blocked. There will be less of a problem if the bridesmaids fan out on the bride's side of the church.

The dignity of the moment is further underlined if the congregation are also asked to stand, but this carries the risk of making the couple less visible to those further back. A compromise that some use is to ask people to remain seated during the Vows, but to stand for the Declarations earlier in the service.

The formal requirement in the rubrics is for the couple to stand before the minister. But if the bride is being 'given away', whoever is doing that will also need to stand, at least until that has happened, and the best man needs to stand until he has handed over the ring(s). In both cases, as with so many other decisions, careful thought is required.

The bride's father, or whoever it is she has chosen, gives the bride's hand to the priest, who will give it to the groom. There are no words in the main text, but the question, 'Who brings this woman to be married to this man?' is in the Notes to the Service – sadly still headed 'the Giving Away'. It no longer says anything that implies that the bride is a piece of goods and chattels and the majority of brides opt for it. But there need be no ceremony, and the *Common Worship* Notes also provide for both sets of parents to entrust their offspring to one other. When there are two fathers – birth-parent and step-parent – this second suggestion can be a useful way of avoiding having to make a choice between them, and in any case reminds us that both parents have an equal part in proceedings.

How the couple say the Vows will have been decided in preparation. The majority prefer to do the traditional thing of repeating the Vows line by line after the priest. Some clergy say the words very quietly as a prompt so that the congregation hear only the words from the couple. But if a couple speak quietly, the Vows may then not be heard at all. Other couples prefer to read the Vows – in which case providing a large-print card is sensible. But that can sound stilted and 'read'. Learning the Vows might sound the most natural of all the alternatives, but it puts a big strain on the couple. I once married a couple who were distinguished members of the Royal Shakespeare Company. I said that I assumed they would be learning their Vows. They recoiled with horror at the very idea, despite the fact that they spent their lives learning far more lines than these. They wanted to enjoy saying them, not remembering them. As with everything else, we should be guided by the couple's wishes and try to accommodate them.

The rubric, 'They loose hands' is a deliberate acting out – he has taken her hand (assuming he has made the first vow – again, something that needs to be decided with each couple). She is his choice. If he keeps tight hold of her whilst she makes her vow, that isn't acting out that it is her free choice as well. It is good if people can see that happening.

The Giving of Rings

If there are two rings, the best man may have both, but some couples prefer one to be handed over by a bridesmaid. After the rings have been blessed, using the form the couple have chosen, they can either be exchanged separately, or after each has put the other's ring on, the words can be said together. That is certainly something that needs to be rehearsed in full, even if there is no rehearsal of the vows. If there is only one ring, then the bride has words of reception to say, so that in either case there is an expression of equality.

The Proclamation

If the congregation are sitting up to this point, some clergy like them to stand now, as the marriage is proclaimed. The holding together of hands is underlined more dramatically when they are wrapped in the stole the priest wears. Most couples have heard the expression 'tying the knot' and are glad to see this being acted out.

Recent films have started a craze for applause from the congregation at this point. Some clergy encourage applause, following the example of bishops who invite congregations to greet the newly-ordained with applause. Others prefer to wait and see what that particular gathering decides to do!

The Blessing of the Marriage

The couple are asked to kneel. If everyone else is standing at this point, it acts out well that the whole people of God are now seeking his blessing on these two people – the only ones not on their feet. It is rather akin to the old ordination services where everyone would stand round the kneeling figure of the person being ordained. It is unfortunate that not all the alternative blessings are reprinted in the *Common Worship* marriage booklet: churches might like to provide couples with all the alternatives so that they can choose the imagery that means most to them.

Making the sign of the cross over the couple at the name of the Trinity, and/or placing a hand on their heads, adds to the solemnity of this formal part of the prayer for them.

The Registration of the Marriage

The text of the service assumes that the registers are signed at this point. This rather presumes that this will take place in church, rather than in the vestry. There is a lot to be said for people being able to see what is going on. Otherwise the signing of the register becomes a time for noisy conversation, and any atmosphere of worship is quickly dissipated. But often decisions such as this are dictated by the shape of the building as much as by the wishes of the couple and theological niceties. If there is a strong reason for signing in the vestry, that is also an argument for moving the registration to the end of the service, after the final hymn and blessing.

The Prayers

In all, 27 alternative prayers are offered in the text of the service, with the added possibilities of the couple choosing other prayers, writing their own, or allowing time for extempore prayer. Much will depend on local custom. Some churches help guide the choices by giving a brief summary of each of the prayers and how they are grouped under headings. You will find a useful example of how to choose the prayers (and also a summary of what each of the readings says) in *Using Common Worship: Marriage* by Stephen Lake (Church House Publishing, 2000).

This is another place in the service where friends and family might be invited to help. If they are asked to lead some or all of the prayers, they will need careful rehearsing.

If the couple already have children, mentioning them by name is important – they too are part of this marriage. The prayers are one opportunity to demonstrate this.

The prayers are usually said at the altar rail, unless there is a nave altar at which the whole service has taken place. The symbolic moving off from the family, who have supported the couple and brought them to this point, to the altar on their first journey as husband and wife has a significance that can be brought out in the marriage preparation.

The prayers end with the Lord's Prayer. A decision about which version to use needs to be made with the couple. These days it is right to include the version chosen in the order of service in case some of those present are not familiar with the version being used – or indeed with either!

The Dismissal

This is a blessing of the whole congregation, not just the couple. At the end of the provision for Marriage within Holy Communion there is an extended blessing based on Numbers 6, and this could be substituted.

The couple walk back up the aisle and the priest is left in the sanctuary, or wherever the blessing has been given. It is good to wait there until the bridal party has reached the back of the church, otherwise the impression can be inadvertently given that you can't wait to go home!

Marriage within Holy Communion

Cranmer intended couples to receive communion at or immediately after their wedding, and the rubrics in *Common Worship* still encourage it for communicant members of the Church. The order is clearly laid out in *Common Worship*, and has excellent material, some of which, like the Peace, might be used in non-eucharistic weddings.

There is an obvious decision to be made about who will receive the sacrament: will it be just the couple or everyone who wishes? Some clergy will not feel comfortable presiding at a service at which an open invitation is not given to all communicants. It can be very moving, if the couple's knees will permit it, for them to remain kneeling at the altar rail whilst their friends and families come forward in turn and join them to receive Holy Communion, or, alternatively, for the couple to sit to one side in the chancel and watch as everyone comes to the altar.

The choice of eucharistic prayer needs some consideration. It is good to use the proper preface(s) that are provided for marriage, but there is also an argument for using Eucharistic Prayer H, which has more for the congregation to join in, and is also very short. Unfortunately, it is not one into which a proper preface can be added.

After the service

Clergy are sometimes generously invited to the reception. Everyone will have their line on whether to accept all, some or none of the invitations. Where it is possible to accept, there are huge opportunities to talk to people whose church connections are very vague. If they have just had a 'good experience' of church, that is an opportunity for mission we should be ready to take. But after any wedding it is possible to mingle with the guests outside church. They may just want to thank you, or comment on the architecture – but sometimes you are providing opportunities for questions that have real significance in their spiritual journeys.

8 And afterwards: getting the follow-up right

This chapter explores the ways in which we can continue to minister to couples and their families after the wedding is over.

The University of Surrey research, referred to on page 23, which gave such positive feedback on what was offered to couples before marriage, painted a very different picture of what happens once the day is over. All but a tiny percentage of couples felt that the church had then lost interest in them. Yet the interest that the few couples experienced and appreciated was nothing spectacular or demanding. The lesson is that we do a considerable disservice by doing nothing, but we can achieve a great deal with even a minimum effort. Keeping a contact, however tenuous, is deeply appreciated.

Keeping in contact

Many churches send anniversary cards, which entails the work of setting up a system. But sending cards can be a significant contribution, and one that, for example, someone who is housebound can make.

One church in the Midlands has taken the anniversary card into a new and much more personal realm. They have a keen digital photographer who takes a close-up of the couple, their transport, the bride's bouquet, and the flowers in church. These are not only published on the parish's web site, but form the basis of a montage that is printed as their anniversary card.

Other churches send a Christmas card for the couple's first Christmas as husband and wife.

Special events

Many churches have special events in national Marriage Week, or St Valentine's-tide (whatever they like to call that time in February). Invitations to special services can go not only to couples who are about to be married, but to those who have recently married. Experience shows that large numbers are willing to come for such an occasion. Some parishes provide refreshments or even a meal after the service. An invitation to bring the photo album to show to others is usually appreciated. The service gives another opportunity to reflect on what marriage is about, and to pray for couples, perhaps by name.

Many churches remember deaths in their intercessions in the 'Year's Mind' – there is no reason why we should not also remember those who married a year ago. Since most marriages are on a Saturday, the first anniversary will be on a Sunday, unless there has been a leap year. An invitation to couples to be in church when they are prayed for is another way to show continued concern and care.

Commendations

In over thirty-five years of ministry, I have only received two commendations from clergy of couples they have married who were moving into the parish where I worked. Commendation of those who move is a sadly neglected aspect of parish life, and those getting married are a significant group who can be helped in this way. It doesn't have to be complicated. It isn't rocket science to keep a pro forma on the computer that says something like:

> *I wish to commend . . . . and . . . . who*
> *recently married in our church, and who live*
> *at . . . . which I believe is in your parish.*
> *They have given me permission to contact you. I hope*
> *someone from your church will be able to visit them,*
> *and that if you have any post-marriage ministry, you*
> *will invite them to take part.*

These days it is probably important to get permission from the couple, but as with so many things, it can best be done in a positive way. They give their future address on the standard marriage application form. The question of getting their assent can easily be covered if on their paperwork there is a statement along the lines of: 'It is our custom to commend couples who get married here to the parish where they will live. Unless you tell us otherwise, we will assume that you are happy for us to do this.'

The other side of the coin is setting up a system for dealing with incoming commendations. What you can offer beyond the important gift of interest in them as people will depend on what else is available locally. Some churches, for example, have a newly-marrieds' group with whom you can put them in touch.

Thanksgiving for Marriage

Common Worship provides an outline order for 'Thanksgiving for Marriage', which can include a Reaffirmation of Vows. Where the service is for everyone, as, for example, in a February service, there would be a general renewal of vows. But there is increasing interest from couples who want to renew vows on a personal basis – maybe not every year, but at regular intervals. Many people are not aware of this possibility, and it can be a seed sown in the minds of a couple at the time of their wedding.

Thanksgiving for Marriage services vary from the very simple, with just the two people present, to full-blown gatherings of the clan to celebrate five, ten, twenty or fifty years of being together. Each anniversary has a traditional gift, and in *Pocket Prayers for Marriage* I refer to these gifts in the prayers I wrote for each of the first ten, and then for every fifth year up to the Golden Wedding. If we take the Marriage Service Preface words seriously – 'Marriage is a sign of unity and loyalty which all should uphold and honour' – then churches have a responsibility to help achieve that, and having frequent anniversary services and making their availability known is part of that contribution.

Ongoing support

Some churches offer follow-up meetings for groups that did marriage preparation together. And some clergy invite couples for a further individual meeting after the wedding. Years ago I did a survey of couples I had married, and asked if they would have liked such a session (which I didn't offer in those days). The vast majority said yes. This has proved a valuable practice. The very first couple I saw had a lot to talk about – one of their parents had died in their first year of marriage. At the end of the session, I noticed the husband getting out his diary. He asked if they could book for the following year. I was slightly taken aback – that hadn't been the plan! But he said that knowing they were coming had encouraged them to think about the good and bad things in the past year, and that had been very helpful to them – so they wanted to make it a regular feature.

In the long term, we need to be able to put couples in touch with people running marriage enrichment courses. These courses may be available locally, or parishes may want to run them for their own couples. My book on using *Growing Together* in groups (see page 29) has a section on how to use the ideas in *Growing Together* for a follow-up course. But there are many experienced groups who provide marriage enrichment courses on a national or regional basis. Some of the addresses are in the Resources list.

9 New opportunities: two case studies

When I set out to write this book, I had thought only in terms of what happens in ordinary parishes, at ordinary weddings. But new and exciting opportunities are opening up because of the growth in the wedding industry. The days when people simply had a choice between their local parish church and the local register office are long gone. All sorts of venues are available for civil marriages, and the Church has been slow to open its mind to the idea of working alongside commercial organizations to provide what some couples, in this consumer-led society, are searching for. Welcoming these new possibilities is over and above any relaxation in the qualifications for where a wedding may take place.

What follows is the example set by two small country parishes, one in Somerset and the other in Leicestershire. Neither is doing anything counter to the regulations as they stand, but they are using those regulations imaginatively, and for the benefit not only of the couples getting married, but also of the local church and, I would argue, the gospel. I am sure there are other examples around the country. Maybe we can be bold enough to look for pro-active openings of this kind.

The beautiful venue: Orchardleigh, Somerset

The parish of Orchardleigh in Somerset has a tiny church built on an island in the grounds of the local stately home. When that was taken over by a new owner in the late nineties, he saw the potential for developing the church as a wedding venue. How right he was is proved by the fact that in 2006 over 60 weddings were held in that church.

But the couples were not resident – and, as we all do, the parish had to explain to them how to qualify. A few opted for residing temporarily in order to get a Superintendent Registrar's Licence, but the majority took the route of attending the church at least once a month for six months in order to be entered on the church electoral roll. For many that involved a drive of two or more hours in each direction – but for some there was an even bigger commitment. One couple commuted from Hong Kong in order to qualify, and another from Belgium. One of the parishes took a register of those attending – they had to sign themselves in at the back of church. The other acted more on trust, but found that this was not abused. Other churches issue couples with a set of dated giving envelopes which acts as an automatic register of attendance.

The popularity of the church was a joy but also a challenge. It is a multi-benefice parish, and when a new incumbent arrived, he was quite reasonably dubious about the time these weddings were taking: it was a disproportionate segment of his ministry. But when he talked of reducing the number of marriages, both the venue and the bishop encouraged him to find ways round the pressures. The bishop, for example, suggested that he involve other local clergy, including those who were in retirement.

The pressures were on others as well – the church has no electricity, and lighting and snuffing the candles for weddings is time-consuming, to say nothing of the necessity to sweep every surface in the church before each service because the bats have made their presence felt! The local organist was in her nineties, and a second organist had to be found for weddings. Happily, one of the churchwardens has taken on the considerable task of doing the administration of the bookings, as well as sometimes pumping the organ.

There is now a move towards employing a part-time administrator, funded from fees charged to the couples. But although these couples pay very large sums to the venue, the church has resisted adding local fees as well and the charges for the verger and organist are less than in many suburban parishes.

Making the most of a mission opportunity: Prestwold, Leicestershire

Similar cooperation with a neighbouring country house has developed very successfully at Prestwold in Leicestershire. But it is low key. The church is mentioned on the venue's literature, but no phone number is given and couples need to attend a service to discuss the possibility of a church ceremony.

The effect of the church services on couples is remarkable. According to one of the incumbents, most of the couples are 'unchurched' – in other words, people who have had no connection with any church in the past. He finds that because they have fewer ideas to undo, they are much more receptive to the Christian message than those who once went to Sunday schools. This is a genuinely 'fresh expression' of church, although within the traditional building.

Local outcomes

The couples enjoy being part of the local communities when they come to worship. One couple in Leicestershire said, 'It's fun to be in your church' – and this a church that regularly uses *The Book of Common Prayer* and says Matins! There have been adult baptisms as a result of people booking a wedding.

The effect on the congregations in both these parishes has been equally positive. Far from feeling invaded, small and struggling communities of largely elderly worshippers have been reinvigorated by these pre-wedding visitors. That is even more important to them than the other obvious benefit of fee income, which helps them pay their way. One of the churchwardens resisted the criticism that the church was being 'used' with the powerful argument that people who would never have darkened a church door were hearing the Christian message, and were having a religious instead of a secular wedding.

We can leave it to God to make use of these openings. What is clear is that without that positive attitude, there simply would not be any openings.

Other local clergy have not been too threatened by these developments – anyway, on the whole, it is not their parishioners who are looking for a wedding elsewhere. The support of bishops in this has been important. The Leicestershire parish writes to the couples' home incumbent(s) with an 'over to you' commendation, which opens up yet more opportunities.

Any wedding preparation for such long-distance couples is inevitably limited. But both churches make valiant attempts to provide for that, and the Leicestershire parish receives free use of the country house twice a year for a marriage preparation day. Both parishes take great care to ensure that things are done well, and that couples get a really positive experience. Their explanatory documents for couples are a model of how it should be done.

What can be done in other places?

Rather than waiting for an approach from the venue, is there not a case for a parish, or indeed a deanery, to make the first move, and ensure that people who want the highest standards of provision for the reception also get the highest standards for the service as well? It will mean educating the civil venues about the labyrinthine rules and regulations we work under in the Church, and it will certainly mean commitment in time and energy, but it is a new way in which we can minister to people who are wanting the very best start to their married life.

10 Radical alternatives: weddings economic, green and ethical

Blowing the whistle on commercialism

The last chapter was about weddings where it often seems money is no object. At the other extreme, the church can also have a fresh approach to weddings. This chapter looks at how people can have a wonderful a day without getting caught up into the 'spend, spend, spend' mentality of the wedding shows.

Parish opportunities

East Anglia seems to lead the way in this respect. For some years, one parish, rather like the National Trust with its free open days, had a couple of days when people could get married in church for free. Of course, that was actually an expense for the parish, because although the parish could waive the fees that it would keep itself, the fees due to the incumbent must be paid to the diocese in the usual way. But it was a way of saying firmly that they didn't want cost to be a reason for not marrying in church.

Using church halls

Very often, finding somewhere to hold the reception is one of the biggest headaches for couples and their families. Are we making the best use of the church halls that many of us have? Who knows, with a keen amateur photographer and someone in the parish with a vintage car, some churches could develop an all-in package that would be really attractive to couples while providing an outlet for the gifts of people within the parish. A deanery in East Anglia has a group of 'Catering Churchwomen' who offer really good receptions in church or village halls at prices that are a fraction of the usual commercial rates.

Refreshments for all

Many years ago I played the organ for a friend's wedding. His bride was Norwegian, and they followed the custom of her country in having coffee and cake at the back of church. When costs of receptions are so high, it is an idea we might want to promote if we have a team of people prepared to help. If everyone can be part of a gathering at church, then the reception afterwards can be for a much smaller group of family and closest friends. Then everyone can meet at the pub in the evening, and buy their own drinks!

Endless possibilities

Once we start thinking 'outside the box', the possibilities are endless. I am grateful to Karen Holford of the Seventh Day Adventist Church, and a former Chair of Churches Together for Families, for permission to include her list of ideas for creating a wedding on a budget. You will find it in Appendix 3.

Ethical, Fair Trade and green weddings

Apart from how to save money, increasingly people are asking questions about how their wedding can save natural resources, and be a blessing not only to them but to God's world.

Almost everything to do with weddings has the potential for being 'green' or 'ethical'. Dresses can be made from fair-traded materials. Food can often be fair-traded. Others will want to go for organically grown food and flowers wherever possible. The invitations and orders of service can be printed on recycled paper.

Many charities now run wedding lists. People already set up in their homes don't need the toasters and mixers of yesteryear. The things the couple *do* need can be ethically sourced. An appealing alternative is to ask for presents that are of benefit to others. As someone commented – giving a camel for a needy farmer is a reminder of the bride-prices of less enlightened times, and is showing love in a practical way. For the amount that people will spend on some weddings, a third-world village could have clean water and help to make itself economically viable for years to come.

In the Resources list, you will find some useful web sites to start you thinking – or type 'ethical weddings' into a search engine. I found over 9,000 links in this country alone.

Appendix 1 Leading people through the service

Preface

The minister reads the Preface, which sets out some of the Church's teaching about marriage.

The Declarations

The minister asks the congregation and the couple if they know any legal impediment to the marriage, and then asks the couple to make their declaration of intent.

The minister says to the congregation

Will you, the families and friends of N and N support and uphold them in their marriage now and in the years to come?

We will.

The Collect

The minister invites the people to pray, silence is kept and the minister says the Collect.

The Vows

The minister introduces the Vows.

N and N, I now invite you to join hands and make your Vows, in the presence of God and his people.

The Giving of Rings

The minister receives the rings, blesses them, and invites the couple to place them on each other's ring finger.

The Proclamation

The minister addresses the people and proclaims the marriage.

The Blessing of the Marriage

The husband and wife kneel, and the minister pronounces the nuptial blessing.

The Dismissal

The minister blesses the congregation.

Appendix 2 A wedding service worksheet

This form is available to download from the FLAME web site at www.flamefamily.co.uk

This sample worksheet was developed for use in a particular parish. It will need adaptation to meet the options available in other places. The page numbers refer to CW Marriage Service. The additional prayers and blessings in CW Pastoral Services are reproduced on sheets for the couple to consult.

MARRIAGE SERVICE WORKSHEET

We want the service as far as possible to include all your personal choices. By filling in the questions on the right-hand side you will gradually compile all the information we need to do that. Take plenty of time over it, and if you are in any doubt, ask the clergy to explain the options next time you see them. The page numbers refer to the copy of the Common Worship Marriage Service booklet. Please delete or write in the answers as appropriate.

Choosing hymns

The most important thing is to choose ones people know and can sing well. There are spaces for four hymns. If you have three hymns, as many do, we omit the one after the Signing of the Registers. If you only want two, we have them at the beginning and the end. Some hymns fit better in one place rather than another – make your list of them all, and discuss with the clergy the order in which we will sing them.

The Prayers

A variety of forms are provided, which you can find in the Additional Prayers Leafet in the folder, or you can write your own – in which case, discuss with the clergy what you have written. Some of the forms cover all four topics suggested within one prayer.
Others are single topic prayers.
There is no 'right' number to use.
What is right for you?

Please include the following:

Which version of the Lord's Prayer?

Thee & thou / You & yours

What hymn will you sing at this point?

Hymn

The Dismissal

What music will you use whilst you walk out of the church?

Music

Appendix 3 Ideas for weddings on a budget

Ideas for themes

Explore wedding traditions from other cultures and choose one or two new ideas to make your wedding extra special.

Look for simple and creative ways to make the wedding memorable rather than expensive and elaborate ways.

Rings

Use the German tradition of wearing the wedding ring on the ring finger of the opposite hand during the engagement.

Buy second-hand rings or use ones handed down through the family.

Buy a simple ring and have a special message engraved inside to personalize it.

Invitations

These can be created attractively and simply using a computer.

To add interest, print on to tracing paper, in grey to look like silver, or in another colour. Punch holes and tie on to folded card in different ways using narrow, coloured ribbons.

Friends skilled in crafts could help to rubberstamp and emboss designs on invitations, or use calligraphy skills that can be photocopied.

Look at all kinds of hand-made cards to find ideas to use in your designs at a fraction of the cost.

The designs can be adapted and used for the programme and the place cards and menu, etc., if needed.

Clothes

Borrow from others.

Buy second hand and sell on again for the same price.

Buy from a charity shop and donate back.

Explore ethnic wedding clothing choices that support Third-World development projects.

Buy clothes that can be worn again later.

Sew wedding clothes for a fraction of the cost, using simple fabrics like cotton and muslin rather than silks and satins.

Flowers

Use the church's flowers from the weekend services, working with the flower arranger on the choice of colours.

Have simple flowers and carry a simple bunch of lilies or daisies with some trailing ivy.

Use silk flower posies that can be reused at other weddings.

Use small trees, such as evergreens or bay trees, that can be decorated with coordinating ribbons and used outside and inside the church, and at the reception, and then be planted in the couple's garden (perhaps these could be a wedding gift from a friend).

After the service, fresh flowers could be given to a nursing home or housebound person.

Music

Ask friends who are musical to play at the service and the reception.

Use a CD player for background music.

Photos

Ask friends to help by taking their own photos, especially anyone with a digital camera, which can be used with a computer to create special effects.

Tape-record the words of the service instead of having a video.

Use a home video rather than a professional photographer.

Ask people to look out for unusual shots to add a fresh dimension to the photographs. Perhaps you could run a competition for the guests, offering a prize for the best wedding photo submitted within a month of the wedding.

Ask someone with a video camera to interview guests about their best memories of the couple, or their favourite relationship tips, etc., to give to the couple, or even to play during the reception.

Transport

Borrow, or use the car of a friend or family member.

Remember that often the car isn't actually seen.

Choose an unusual form of transport, or even a taxi.

If the church is local, walk there with a parade of friends all holding tall colourful flowers, such as gladioli.

The friends can make an arch of flowers for the couple, or bride alone, to walk under into the church.

Hair

Choose a simple style that you can do yourself, and add fresh flowers for a special look.

Food

Organize friends to bring donated dishes to provide a buffet.

Buy food from a wholesale food outlet to make catering easy and cut costs.

Serve just cake, drinks and nibbles.

Serve an agape meal using fruits, nuts, breads and other simple foods.

Invite friends to bring a bottle.

Use glasses loaned from friends – make a small mark underneath with a waterproof pen to indicate whose glasses are whose so that they can be returned later.

For tablecloths, use plain white sheets that can be given to the couple as a wedding present.

Use ivy and wild flowers in abundance to provide simple and free table decorations.

Cake

Purchase ready-made and iced cakes from a supermarket.

Use one small, decorated cake, and cut up ready-made cakes for serving.

Decorate cakes with curled ribbons, lace, or fresh flowers for a quick and simple stylish finish.

Decorate cakes using simple shapes, such as hearts or ivy leaves, cut from rolled icing with a shaped cutter.

Explore the wedding cakes used by other cultures and see if something else appeals to you.

Wedding

Do something at the wedding that will inspire and encourage other married couples.

Encourage other couples to reaffirm vows.

Hand out small cards with encouragement for married couples.

Pass around a blank book for guests to write in their best tips for a happy marriage, or ideas for special nights out.

Create a special presentation on PowerPoint for the wedding service or reception to add something unique to the event – this could be emailed to friends who couldn't come.

Churches

Be eco-friendly by providing simple decorations that can be used at weddings.

Provide stain resistant, easy-care white tablecloths that can be used for special occasions.

Develop a loan service for many items needed for weddings to help couples cut the cost.

Work together as a community to create special weddings for couples attending the church.

Resources list

Books and leaflets

General

Body, Andrew and Pippa (compilers), *Pocket Prayers for Marriage*, Church House Publishing, 2004.

Thatcher, Adrian (ed.), *Celebrating Christian Marriage*, T & T Clark, 2001.

Your marriage in the Church of England (leaflet), Church House Publishing (available in packs of 20).

Liturgical

Common Worship: Services and prayers for the Church of England, Church House Publishing, 2000.

Church House Publishing, *Common Worship: Marriage*, 2000.

Church House Publishing, *Common Worship: Pastoral Services*, 2000, 2nd edition 2004.

Lake, Stephen, *Using Common Worship: Marriage*, Church House Publishing, 2000.

Marriage preparation resources

Body, Andrew, *Growing Together*, Church House Publishing, 2005.

Body, Andrew, *Growing Together: the Course*, Church House Publishing, forthcoming.

Visual Liturgy, Church House Publishing. This is a software package to help people plan services and acts of worship using a computer.

Holy Trinity Brompton Marriage Preparation course: information about this course may be found at **www.themarriagecourse.org**

Display materials

Some Diocesan communication officers have a wide experience of shows and may be able to give advice. For example Gillian Oliver (gillian.oliver@c-of-e.org.uk) is working with the communications officers of the dioceses on this. Some social responsibility officers and FLAME groups have also had stands at fairs, for example in the Diocese of Canterbury and the Diocese of Gloucester (francescatolond@yahoo.co.uk). Sue Burridge at the Archbishops' Council can also give assistance and provide display stands for groups to borrow (sue.burridge@ c-of-e.org.uk).

Web resources

Ethical and green weddings

www.alternativeweddinglist.co.uk

www.cat.org.uk

www.ethicalweddings.com

www.greatgifts.org/giftselection/weddinglists.aspx

www.greenweddings.org.uk

www.oxfamunwrapped.com/weddinglistinfo.aspx

Hymns and readings

www.weddingguide.co.uk/articles/wordsmusic/
hymns/hymnsforyourservice.asp (This one offers midi files
so you can hear them)

www.2-in-2-1.co.uk/tips/wedhymns.html

www.cofe.anglican.org/lifeevents/weddings/
musicreadings.html

Liturgy

The Church of England liturgy web site

www.cofe.anglican.org/worship/liturgy/commonworship/texts/
marriage/marriagefront.html

Marriage sites

The Association for Marriage Enrichment
www.ame-uk.org.uk

Care for the Family
www.careforthefamily.org.uk

Churches Together for Families
www.churchesandfamilies.org

FLAME (The Family Life and Marriage Education Network)
www.flamefamily.co.uk

The FOCCUS Marriage Inventory
www.foccus.co.uk

The Mothers' Union
www.mothersunion.org.uk